INTRODUCING EXTENDED SAXOP TECHNIQUES

CW00419474

By Curtis Macdonald

AUDIO CONTENTS

1	VOWELS	20	'CROW' PITCHES A
2	PORTAMENTO	21	'CROW' PITCHES B
3	'QUARTER' TONES	22	RHYTHMIC KEY CLICKS
4	RHYTHMIC VIBRATO	23	CIRCULAR BREATHING
5	ARTICULATION PRACTICE 1	24	PREPARATIONS
6	ARTICULATION PRACTICE 2	25	LOW A
7	SLAP TONGUE 1		
8	SLAP TONGUE 2		
9	SLAP TONGUE 3		
10	SUB-TONES		
11	OVERTONES 1		
12	MULTIPHONICS 1		
13	OVERTONES 2		
14	OVERTONES COMBINED		
15	MULTIPHONICS 2		
16	VOCALIZATIONS A		
17	VOCALIZATIONS B		
18	VOCALIZATIONS C		
19	VOCALIZATIONS D		

1 2

Visit us on the Web at www.melbay.com — E-mail us at email@melbay.com.

TABLE OF CONTENTS

....

This book is dedicated to all of my teachers, whose guidance has enabled me to share the practice of music and sound, both heard and unheard.

PREFACE

The saxophone, like all wind instruments, is inspired and influenced by the human voice. As such, there lies an enormous potential for the production of sound, and a great responsibility falls upon the instrumentalist to fully master the nuances of his or her instrument. By studying the extended techniques of the saxophone, we open ourselves to a very subtle and delicate process of fine-tuning our instrumental abilities, which results in the discovery of new resonances and sonic prowess.

It is not necessary to perform any extended techniques in order to benefit from them. Think of these techniques as a form of cross training for the saxophone. Most importantly, the practice of extended techniques is a practice of focus, balance and patience. These exercises are designed to help cultivate the subtle skills of refining saxophone sound, and do not exclude any particular musical style or aesthetic. The exercises do not come from any one particular methodology or school of thought. Instead, the ideas presented here are designed to help unlock a deeply unique and personal approach to saxophone practice. Therefore, these practices can be viewed as a holistic and yet a practical approach to developing an advanced instrumental proficiency, while at the same time building a very intimate, individualized sonic palette for creative use. Cultivating this internal, introspective practice is key to developing the highest musical expression through the saxophone.

Practice these exercises in addition to any other instrumental studies you are currently pursuing. This book is not a complete method for learning the saxophone by itself, and it does not try to replace the ancient relationship between mentor and apprentice. Working closely with a qualified instructor is of paramount importance to becoming the best musician that you can be. The intention here is to supplement one's regular practice with these exercises; the result will be a greater aural awareness and an expanded command of the instrument.

PREREQUISITES

As a prerequisite, the author assumes that the instrumentalist has at least an intermediate understanding of the mechanics of the saxophone, including being able to consistently produce a stable embouchure and air column at will, throughout the conventional range of the instrument. Additionally, the author assumes that the instrumentalist knows basic music theory conventions, such as all major and minor scales along with their respective modes, and can read music at an intermediate level, so that the author can properly convey the intended nature of each exercise expressed within this book.

It should be noted that the mouthpiece and reed setup plays a role in the responsiveness of some of these techniques. For example, a stiff reed in combination with a large mouthpiece tip opening accounts for added difficulty when practicing the overtone series and multiphonics, and proves to be more challenging for executing certain articulations, such as the slap-tongued articulation effects. Therefore, it is wise to strive for a balance between tip opening and reed stiffness, and choose a setup that facilitates a comfortable and free-blowing dynamic range. One shouldn't harbor any tension in the head just from playing and holding a mid-range concert B♭, for instance. If you are experiencing tension in the head, neck or shoulders after playing for only a few minutes, it is advisable to search for a more 'playable' setup.

Every saxophone is different, and some techniques that are easily available on one instrument, i.e. the tenor saxophone, may not be as readily available when brought to another, say, the alto saxophone. Also, a saxophonist who has switched from playing a modern instrument to a vintage instrument, or vice versa, may find that certain mechanics and resonances function completely differently. Changes like this are unavoidable and show us that the unique properties of each instrument will have an effect on how successful certain exercises will be. That being said, by embracing the limitations of your physicality and your instrument's design, you may find an altogether new and exciting frontier of possibilities to explore, which may become a defining part of your sound.

Like every saxophone, every saxophonist is unique as well. This book offers ideas to explore on your instrument, but is by no means an ultimatum or encyclopedic resource of extended technique procedure. In almost all cases, I urge you to improvise your own exercises based on these ideas in order to further explore the 'sound within the sound'. Those little 'noises' that are embedded deep within the resonance are the gateways into a new palette of sound. Please combine all of these exercises with your regular conventional saxophone practice for the sake of balance and wholeness. The goal is to enable you, dear reader, with all of the tools to develop a strong foundation for an expressive saxophone performance.

KEEP YOUR CHIN UP

There will be at times frustration along this journey since the practice of any new, unconventional technique can be quite humbling. Many months of hard work can go by without seeing much progress, but this is to be expected when we are learning something new. Try to have a sense of humor with your struggles. Laugh out loud when you're surprised by a sudden 'squeak' or 'squawk', and take joy with the experience of trying something unfamiliar. The most important thing to remember is to stay focused, and change up what and how you're practicing by a little bit each day in order to keep your practice fresh and interesting. Be patient, and know that all of these techniques are very much within your reach. If you practice with a little focus and patience each day, everything will come to you very, very quickly.

It is advisable to limit one's practice to just one or two of these techniques per day, and practice for a small but focused period of time. Each chapter in this book is a world unto itself. Play with the examples, and then make your own. 20 minutes of quality practice a day is enough to see measurable progress in just one week. Regardless of how long you practice, be sure to take several micro-breaks of 30 to 45 seconds in duration every 5 minutes or so in order to regroup, relax and recover one's focus over both body and mind. During these little rest periods is where the practice begins to grow.

Please feel welcome to skip over entire chapters or skim through several ideas until you find something that's interesting to work on. Also feel free to spend several weeks focusing in on just one exercise and really get inside of it; it's all part of the learning process. Encourage yourself with good practice habits: practice often and stay awake.

THE SECRET

The practice of extended techniques is an introspective practice that alters the experience of playing the saxophone. With this in mind, mastering a subtle, 'microscopic' control over these three physical elements will unlock all possibilities:

1) Vowels/Throat-shape
2) Lip pressure/Embouchure; and,
3) Airspeed/Dynamics.

This is what we will be working on in the pages ahead.

BREATHING

It is part of a wind instrumentalist's practice to review the fundamentals of sound production. For us, this means spending a short time reflecting on the quality of your breathing.

There are three main 'chambers' to a full breath:

1) The first and largest chamber of a full breath is located in your abdominals. As your breathe in, allow your belly to fully expand in all directions. This chamber should contain about 60% of your breath.

2) The second chamber of the breath is located in your ribcage and is associated with your heart and chest. As you continue to breathe in, allow your ribs to expand to their fullest expression. This chamber should contain about 30% of your breath.

3) The third and smallest chamber of the breath is at the very top of your torso, where your chest meets your shoulders. Complete your inhale and let the air rise up into the top of your chest easily and naturally. This chamber should contain about 10% of your breath.

Together, these three parts to the breath define what a full inhale can feel like. Practice by inhaling slowly and consciously, focusing on how each chamber expands. On the exhale, focus on a reverse-order release beginning at the top of your chest. Practice this slowly, and for five complete breaths.

....

Then modify your practice ever so slightly: Pause briefly at the top of an inhale to experience what it feels like to be completely 'full'. Pause at the bottom of an exhale to experience the feeling of emptiness. Do this five more times, slowly and in control. This time try closing your eyes.

A breathing practice like this will help energize your body and mind before you approach your horn. If it is a cold, wintery day, breathing like this will also help to warm you up very quickly.

....

Not sure if you're breathing properly? Do you feel like you're holding your breath when you're playing? Try this:

Lie down with your back on the floor, legs stretched out in front of you. If your lower back is sensitive, place your feet on the floor so that your legs are bent. Place your left hand at the center of your chest, between your ribs just above your sternum, where your heart is. Place your right hand on your belly button Take deep breaths, let out a few sighs, and then breathe normally. Observe how your breath changes. Where does it start? Where does it end? What hand rises when? How high does it rise? Investigate this for 10 to 20 full breaths. Self-observation is the best teacher we have.

....

To further build physical and mental awareness for your breathing, consider pursuing breath-conscious, extra-curricular physical activities such as swimming, yoga, or Pilates, all of which require a steady focus on the breath, and build core abdominal strength.

THE CHIN PUSH-UP EXERCISE

This is an exercise to build superior control and strength in your embouchure. In this exercise, there are two chin positions to focus on: a 'straight' chin, which is a downward position; and a 'bunched' chin, which is a upward position. We will not need the instrument for the first part of this exercise.

Begin by gently curling both top and bottom lips over your top and bottom teeth, respectively. Hold both top and bottom lips together using gentle pressure from your jaw. This will be our neutral position. Be sure to keep your jaw stationary; keep your lips sealed and do not move your jaw away from this position.

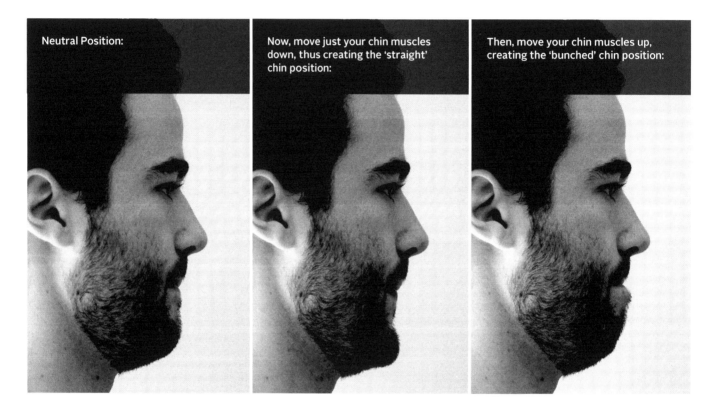

Neutral Position:

Now, move just your chin muscles down, thus creating the 'straight' chin position:

Then, move your chin muscles up, creating the 'bunched' chin position:

Continue practicing this movement back and forth, up and down, isolating only the muscles of your chin. Remember to not move your lips or jaw at all. Within a few repetitions, you should begin to feel the heat and intensity build. When this happens, you'll know that you're building the strength for optimum embouchure flexibility and control.

Now bring this exercise to the instrument. Play and hold a steady tone for as long as possible, going back and forth from holding a straight chin, then a bunched chin; then a straight chin, then a bunched chin, again and again. Be patient, diligent, and check yourself in a mirror for the correct chin placement. Be extreme with your positions to help ingrain the experience.

Know that if you are smiling while you're playing, you have the perfect embouchure: relaxed and yet strong and focused. Remind yourself of this many times as you read on.

The shape of the throat and the position of the tongue dramatically affect the resonant quality of sound, which is something we experience as 'timbre'. This chapter is a practice of resonance awareness. To begin, we will focus on sounding just the vowels themselves, away from the instrument.

UH OO OH AH EYE AYE EE

Sing a single tone, and project a clear and focused tone steadily as you gradually change through the following vowels:

very slowly sing:

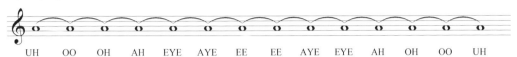

What do you hear? What do you feel? Is there a vowel that is more 'wide' than another? Or one that is more 'narrow'? Which vowel sounds bright? Which sounds dark? Sing them again and again. Soak in the sounds.

While you're slowly cycling through the vowels, are you hearing anything that's changing? What is your tongue doing in each of these vowels? Where is it 'going'? Keep singing.

Now try holding a single vowel sound, perhaps over the vowel AH, but change the position of your tongue. This time try moving the tongue towards the top of your mouth while holding the vowel AH. Do you hear how the resonance is changing as you change your tongue position? Listen closely, and patiently. Marinate in the changing timbre.

Now try focusing in on just two or three vowels of your own choosing, and feel how they morph in to, and out of, each other. Observe your tongue, where is it? Is there a position it favors? If you move it, in what way does its movement affect the sound of the resulting harmonics?

Sing in an octave that comfortably suits your voice. Keep your jaw relaxed and avoid moving it much as you slowly cycle through vowels. Take in deep and soothing inhales, and project your voice as if it were coming from your heart and throat (instead of thinking it coming merely from your mouth). Also spend some time humming the vowels, so that you can still make shape adjustments inside your throat. Take note of how your tongue behaves.

Finally, bring this practice to the saxophone by holding a single note, and slowly change the vowel and throat-shape:

play:

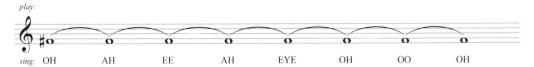

Then, play a few different intervals on the saxophone in simple harmony, like octaves and 5ths and explore what each new vowel brings to the sound:

play:

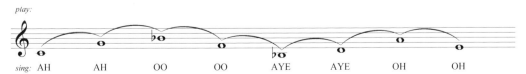

PORTAMENTO EXERCISE

Portamento is the term for sliding from one note to the next. This is an exercise designed to gain complete control over the movement of your fingers on the keys.

Close your eyes. Imagine your hands were suspended in a thick molasses. Try to feel what the spring tension of each key feels like against your hand in complete detail. Avoid any sudden fingering movements; instead, pretend like you are playing in slow motion, gently gliding from one note to the next. Avoid changing anything in your embouchure; make sure it is relaxed, calm and neutral as this is not an exercise for your jaw or lips. Do not tongue during this exercise. Try to slur every note, and with that little observer in your mind, check to see if your wrists and fingers are over-gripping keys or harboring any tension. If they are, take a break and mindfully release your hands away from the instrument.

Experience the slow and gentle timing and movement to and from each fingering. For example, practice the following passage, breathing where necessary:

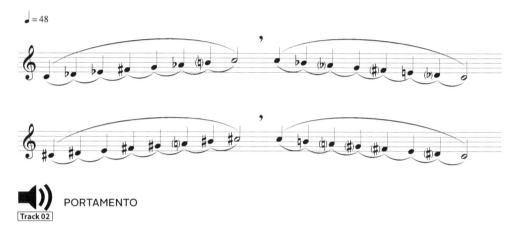

PORTAMENTO
Track 02

This exercise, when practiced correctly, should feel very smooth and fluid in your hands. Avoid any gripping the keys at all costs. If you are having difficulty with keeping a fluid sensation in your hands, you may also practice this in front of a mirror and check to see if your fingernails are turning white. If so, immediately take your hands off the instrument and remind yourself of the intention to stay relaxed and focused, without holding any tension in your fingers, hands or wrists, or anywhere else in your body for that matter. The more delicately you practice this exercise, that is, the more you 'zoom-in' and hang out in the space in-between the notes, the more you will learn.

....

This 'slow-motion' portamento exercise can be applied to any étude or selection of music. Think of this exercise as a method of microscopically observing the physical nuances between your fingers, the desired pitches, and the spring tension of each key's depression and release. As with all of the exercises in this book, cultivating the feeling of steady, balanced focus is our goal.

FINGERINGS THAT ALTER PITCH AND TIMBRE

The saxophone can be used to alter the pitch and timbre of certain tones. This is accomplished by venting the air differently through the horn, which requires us to adopt some unconventional fingerings. Below is a fingering chart of some of these alternative fingerings, organized 'chromatically' from lowest to highest sounding tone.

In this chapter, fingerings illustrated in boxes are conventional fingerings you already know. The fingerings that are not in boxes are those that produce the 'notes in between the notes'. Note: Shaded-in keys denote half-pressed keys.

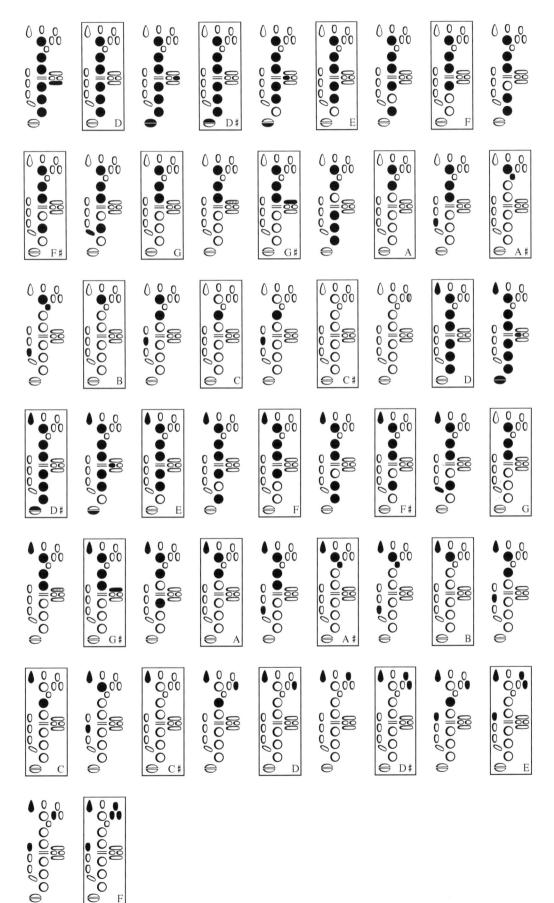

Now apply some of these fingerings in the context of a musical passage:

Track 03 'QUARTER' TONES

Now try improvising some melodies using these fingerings, taking this moment to lavish in the new intervallic possibilities you just created for yourself.

....

Sometimes these altered fingerings are generally referred to as 'quarter-tone fingerings'. Please take this labeling with a grain of salt because even at its best, quarter-tonality on the saxophone is very much approximated since there are few and far between pure quartertone fingerings available, and the faintest adjustment of our embouchure can render a quartertone fingering into something that it isn't.

Take this opportunity to find some other fingerings that produce alternative tones and pitches. Make note of these fingerings in the blank diagrams below.

Here's a tip to get you started: Begin on a conventional fingering, and then try closing or opening some other key(s) that are not typically associated with that particular fingering. Keep trying different combinations and record your observations. These fingerings can be a great new resource for various stylistic ornamentations that you may find useful in performance.

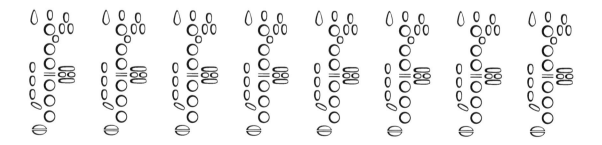

RHYTHMIC VIBRATO

Vibrato is a phased, pitch bend effect. By ever so slightly lowering one's jaw away from a neutral position on the reed (and returning it back again) we produce a single pulse of vibrato. In this chapter we will practice a controlled, rhythmic note-bending exercise, or what we will refer to as a 'rhythmic vibrato'.

The main prerequisite to this chapter is to be able to produce a steady, focused tone for at least the duration of a full breath. It is a good idea to begin practicing with a straight tone, before adding vibrato to the sound.

Begin by setting the metronome to a very slow tempo. For this first example, set it one quarter-note equal to 60 beats per minute (♩ = 60). Start by sounding a pure, vibrato-less tone for several beats, and then begin to induce vibrato with steady 'depth' or 'width' to the pulsations, maintaining pure rhythmic consistency for as long as possible, without building up any tension in the jaw, lips or throat. Keep your embouchure relaxed. Then change the pulsing rhythm as demonstrated here:

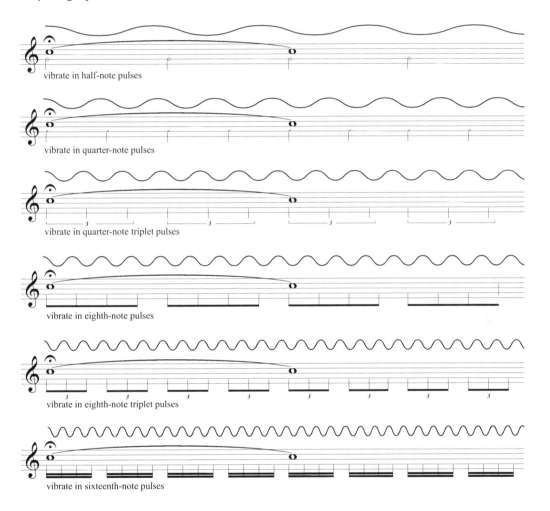

Continue to practice a complete range of rhythms, from dramatically slow vibrato pulses (noting how subtly it changes the sound between each pulsation), to a quick 'spinning' sound while maintaining control and a consistent depth to the pulses. Try this exercise on several pitches, observing how the vibrato changes as you go higher and lower in pitch, throughout the range of the horn.

After you've mastered this, practice smoothly transitioning from a very shallow, narrow vibrato to a very deep, broad range of vibrato, while varying the rhythm, and at different tempos. For example:

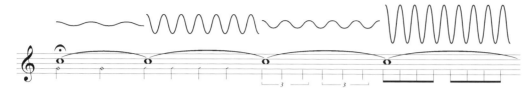

Practice in this manner across many different pitches, octaves, and in several dynamic ranges: *pp*, *mf*, and *ff*.

Finally, improvise vibrating tones in various depths, tempos and rhythms, throughout the range of the horn. For example:

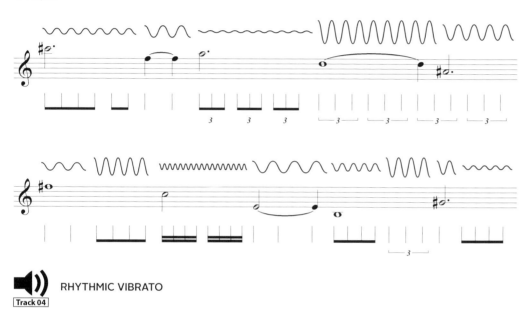

🔊 **RHYTHMIC VIBRATO**
Track 04

Please note that one must maintain an awareness to avoid any 'biting' of the embouchure during this exercise. There mustn't be any pain. If you notice yourself biting your lip and teeth against the reed, or if your lip starts to hurt after a few minutes, please take the opportunity to pause your practice, in order to regain a sense of relaxedness. If the problem persists, leave the exercise for the day and come back around to it tomorrow. You've done great work already.

ARTICULATION

Preparing one's throat and tongue properly is a necessary skill that is key to unlocking many extended techniques, and the practice of vibrato and tongue control goes a very long way in support of this development.

Here are some basic, yet powerful articulation warm-up exercises. The syllable for producing a basic, 'tongued' articulation is to simply produce a "tah" sound on the reed. Each one of these articulation patterns can be applied to any musical passage, étude, or exercise endlessly:

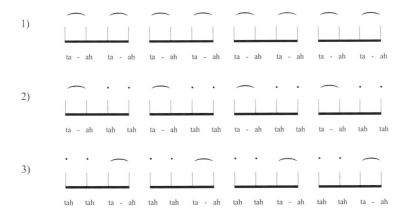

The above articulation patterns applied to a chromatic scale:

 ARTICULATION PRACTICE 1

Track 05

Now, practice the same exercise but add a more aggressive staccato to each articulation. Let the sound of the syllable "Tuht!" be your guide.
The above articulation patterns applied to a major scale:

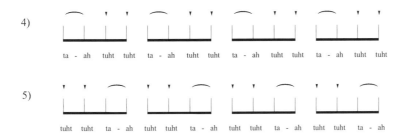

 ARTICULATION PRACTICE 2

Track 06

While applying these articulations to a musical example, go back and forth between practicing with staccato and staccatissimo. Doing so will build up more strength in your tongue and will prepare you to explore deeper into other areas of articulation. For example, the more aggressive staccatissimo articulation leads itself into the practice of slap-tonguing, of which there are a few techniques to be made aware of.

A hard-slap tongue is executed as a violent, single strike upon the reed produced by a sudden burst of air—quickly released by the jaw, which drops off the mouthpiece as a result. A hard-slap tongue produces a sound with very little tonal information, and is generally very explosive and percussive sounding:

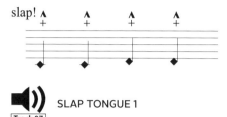

 SLAP TONGUE 1

A soft-slap tongue is an articulation of the tongue that intercepts air quickly passing through the mouthpiece while at the same time preventing the reed from vibrating. This is achieved by thinking of producing the syllable "HUT" into the mouthpiece, with emphasis on a hard "T" sound. This produces a sound effect that is both percussive and tonal. Many discreet, fingered tones can be heard when slap-tonguing using this technique.

 SLAP TONGUE 2

A medium-hard slap tongue has the characteristics of both hard and soft-slap tongue effects, and can be accomplished by very quickly producing the syllable "T'HUT!" into the instrument.

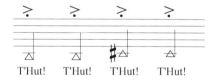

SLAP TONGUE 3

Apply some of these slap-tongue articulations to several musical passages of your own choosing in a variety of tempos, being sure to never sacrifice the articulation's quality for speed. There is much to be learned from applying new articulations to some music that you are working on, substituting the notated articulations for your own.

When practicing slap tonging, aim for a consistent sound throughout the several registers. Be sure to check yourself against a slow, metronomic pulse to cultivate rhythmic accuracy and a sense of endurance.

....

After you feel comfortable executing a few slap tongues consistently, replace the articulation in the staccato and staccatissimo examples on page X with patterns of slap tongue articulations. For example:

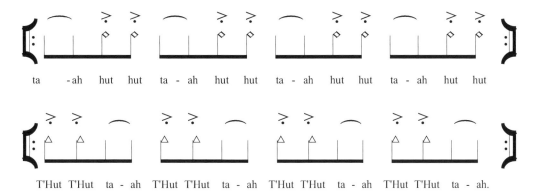

ta -ah   hut   hut   ta - ah   hut   hut   ta - ah   hut   hut   ta - ah   hut   hut

T'Hut T'Hut ta - ah   T'Hut T'Hut ta - ah   T'Hut T'Hut ta - ah   T'Hut T'Hut ta - ah.

THE SUB-TONE EFFECT

The sub-tone is a soft, warm sounding effect easiest to execute on the lower register of the horn. To create this effect we must lightly 'bunch' up our chin muscles (like we did for the chin push-up exercise), and slightly drop our jaw (unlike the chin push-up exercise). This way, we create a wide "nozzle" with our throat and embouchure, which allows the air to flow out more slowly. Think of sounding the vowel "UH" with a loose jaw. This will move your tongue forward in your mouth, and open up the back of your throat.

Practice going back and forth between a normal tone and sub-tones on tones that fall below the break of the octave key. Keep in mind that sounding a normal tone requires a faster airspeed than a sub-tone. Essentially, this practice is an exercise of varying degrees of airspeed.

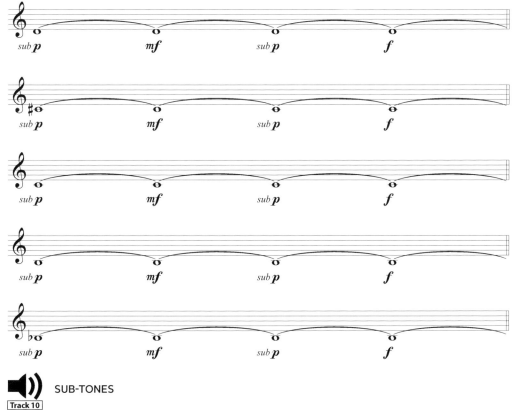

🔊 SUB-TONES
Track 10

15

After you feel comfortable subtoning in the lower register, expand your practice by applying a subtone practice to the middle, middle-high and high registers in order to see what new timbres you can gain control of.

OVERTONES, PART I

The natural harmonics of the saxophone (also known as 'overtones') are very special. This practice enables you to experience the saxophone as a pure and resonant, harmonious object. By experiencing and identifying the subtle nuances between each of the harmonics, we gain both the insight and the capacity to traverse into another world of sound.

The secret to correctly executing these exercises is to slowly and carefully change your throat's vowel shape as practiced earlier on page 7. As you apply these vowels, practice observing how different throat shapes affect how the overtones 'speak'. Combine this observation with a focus of adjusting your airspeed—sometimes increasing it, sometimes decreasing it, and sometimes holding it steady throughout these practices. And please be careful. There is a tendency to 'bite' or 'clamp' one's jaw and embouchure too tightly the higher one gets up the harmonic series. Please be reminded that a sense of balance is what we are looking for. If your physicality feels unbalanced, take your hands off the instrument and regroup by singing a few vowels slowly away from the instrument for a moment.

Most importantly, keep your focus tuned-in on these five things when working on any overtonal exercise:

1) Hold the sound steady on a single harmonic.

2) Make just a small vowel/throat-shape adjustment in order to move from one harmonic to the next.

3) Play a few of the harmonics in the same breath, staying relaxed, focused and in control of the sound.

4) Practice with a gentle articulation (tongued), and also without any articulation (slurred).

5) Practice slowly and patiently.

The dashed line indicates staying on the fundamental fingering (in this case, a low B♭), while at the same time sounding the natural harmonic above.:

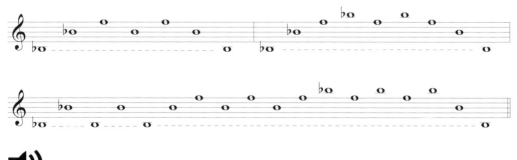

🔊 OVERTONES 1

Track 11

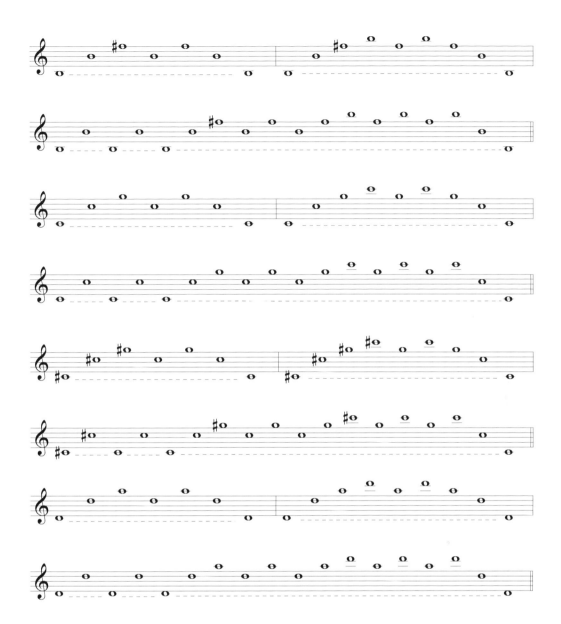

It should be mentioned that after a thorough practice of overtones, one would naturally gain the ability to play high pitches above the range of the instrument. The pitches that are above the conventional range of the instrument are referred to as belonging to the 'altissimo' register. I have intentionally left out of this book a chapter on altissimo fingerings, as I believe there is more than enough common resource available online to discover various altissimo fingerings for you and your instrument. Whatever your inclination may be to pursue the highest range of the saxophone, know that all altissimo fingerings are of secondary importance to having a fluid command over the natural harmonics of the horn. If you are finding yourself struggling with any altissimo fingering, or if you simply cannot find the right ones, please revisit the study of the overtones and a clearer experience and understanding will undoubtedly begin to surface.

....

Bonus practice: Want to try something adventurous and challenging? Play a piece of music without using the octave key, using only your throat to play in the higher octaves!

Inducing multiple tones on the instrument is quite challenging, and requires a heightened sensitivity and control between all the elements of saxophone mechanics: vowel/throat-shape, lip pressure/embouchure position and airspeed/dynamics. Add to the mix a collection of unconventional fingerings that drastically create instability in the air column. On a monophonic instrument, we are attempting to produce polyphony, which is somewhat of a paradox. We are seeking stability on unstable territory. This is very tricky and takes much practice.

Determining what fingerings work and do not work for you is part of the practice. Please know that ANY fingering (even conventional fingerings) can produce a multiphonic if sculpted with the appropriate attention in one's throat shape, embouchure and airspeed.

Some multiphonic fingerings work better in lower registers than in the higher ones. To determine what works best, carefully adjust your throat shape slowly and gradually to find out what register is most conducive to a particular fingering.

Here are some introductory multiphonic fingerings. Practice these until you feel stable in each one, and can attack each multiphonic clearly across a variety of articulations: accented (>), staccato (•), legato (—) etc.

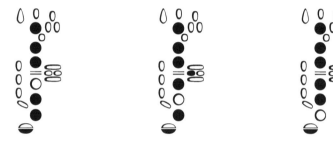

Then continue your practice by moving slowly and smoothly between two different multiphonic fingerings in the same breath, as indicated by the arrows, in much the same way we practiced the portamento exercise on page 8.

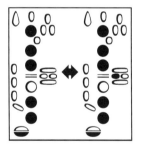
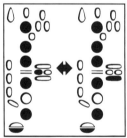
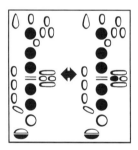

 MULTIPHONICS 1
Track 12

When you are comfortable producing the above multiphonics, here is another small set of fingerings to explore:

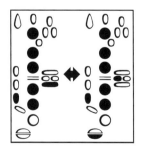
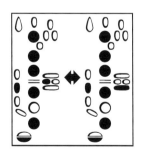
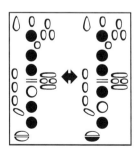

Practice these multiphonics with as much control as possible. Allow each multiphonic to emerge slowly and gracefully from one to another. It's okay if you play the fingering and don't sound a multiphonic at first. Let the sound marinate a little. Accept whatever sound comes out first. Play the fingering, and then make only the faintest adjustment of your throat, embouchure and/or airspeed, and observe what begins to emerge. Let this be a practice of delicate balance. And also be sure to practice sounding these multiphonic sounds with these dynamics in mind:

$$ppp < p \qquad pp < mp \qquad pp < mf \qquad mp < f \qquad mf < ff$$

Multiphonic Dynamic Set 1:
Now revisit the fingerings on page 9 where we practice 'the notes in between the notes'. Do any of these fingerings double as multiphonic fingerings? Can you find new multiphonic fingerings by modifying a fingering by just one key? Try a few out for yourself, and record your findings in the blank fingerings below:

Fill in the holes to create your own multiphonic fingering pairs:

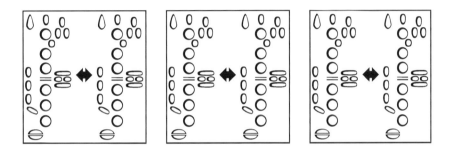

....

OVERTONES, PART II

Here are some more involved practices of the natural harmonics of the saxophone. Please be patient with these exercises, and take refuge in knowing that you will gain the most benefit from these exercises by practicing them slowly, and with a sense of ease and relaxedness. Know that it's perfectly acceptable to practice just a few overtones, or only a small fragment of these examples at a time.

Note: The dashed line indicates the fundamental fingering to hold while sounding the harmonics.

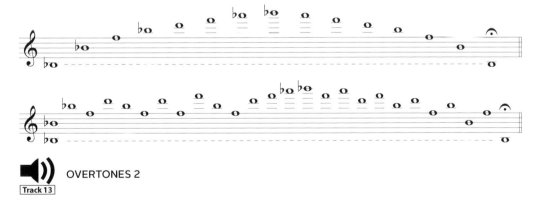

🔊 OVERTONES 2

Track 13

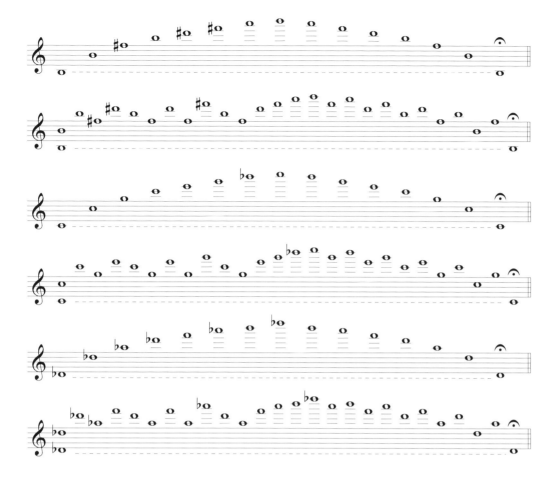

This is big work, and I applaud you for all your hard work and dedication. Know that it will pay off immensely. You will feel your sound beginning to change and get deeper. If you are thirsty for more, practice the above exercise again, but this time read the examples backwards (in retrograde).

....

Now we will combine the harmonics of different generating tones to create melodies by only using overtones. The examples below outline the beginning of such a practice. After you have a handle on these few examples, be sure to try improvising some of your own overtonal melodies.

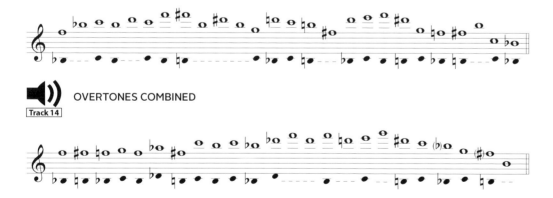

OVERTONES COMBINED

Track 14

Continue to practice some of your own invented melodies over the 5 lowest fundamental tones: B, C, C ♯ (or D♭) and D:

Be sure to take a moment after all these overtones to make sure you are still relaxed in your embouchure. Oftentimes it helps to apply a subtle rhythmic vibrato to the higher harmonics to help us relax our jaw and lip:

If you're finding that you're over-blowing a little, or if it just seems too loud after a while of overtone practice, consider practicing with a set of earplugs. (I recommend every musician owning a set of professionally fitted 'musician's earplugs' also known as 'filters' among audiologists). Practicing while wearing earplugs changes your perspective and how you hear your sound, which is always a worthwhile experiment. Wearing earplugs when playing a wind instrument reveals the sound of what's happening in your mouth and throat, in particular the movement of your throat and tongue. I encourage you to try it out for yourself. In our extended technique practice, this perspective change may be a helpful tool that can help us expose and correct a few little bad habits orally.

Here are some more multiphonic fingerings to explore on your instrument. These multiphonics are more unstable than the first ones we explored, and as such, there is more resistance in the air column to counteract. Sometimes, in order to produce these multiphonics we must drastically change our throat shape and airspeed. In other cases, we must loosen our embouchure beyond what feels normal. Sometimes the adjustment we must make is incredibly subtle. Find your balance and ease into each sound. During practice, take a moment every once in a while to completely release your hands from the instrument and shake them out. Oftentimes we over-grip these new fingerings after holding them for a while.

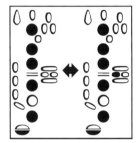 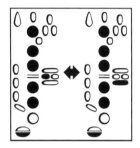 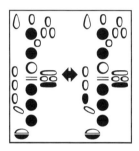

 MULTIPHONICS 2
Track 15

(Play this one as quietly as possible, like a subtone.)

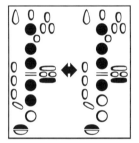 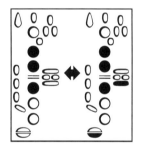 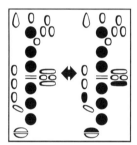

As you progress in your practice, explore implementing different articulations, vibrato and these other dynamics to your multiphonics. If you are struggling with sounding a particular multiphonic fingering, oftentimes it could mean that you are not quite playing at the optimum dynamic range for that multiphonic. Practice observing how the shape of your throat changes, as if you were playing in a different register than the fingering suggests. Explore this sensation while you practice multiphonics through the following dynamic sets:

Multiphonic Dynamic Set 1:

$$ppp < p \qquad pp < mp \qquad pp < mf \qquad mp < f \qquad mf < ff$$

Multiphonic Dynamic Set 2:

$$f > mp \qquad ff > mf \qquad sffz < mp \qquad sffz < mf \qquad sffz < f$$

Here are some additional multiphonic fingerings to investigate on your instrument:

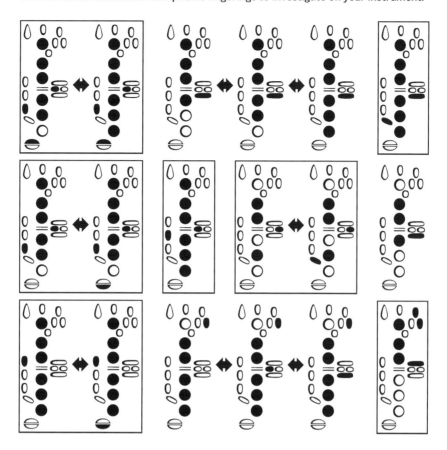

Be sure to try out different jaw positions. Sometimes a relaxed lower lip and open throat, (like a sub-tone embouchure) helps produce a multiphonic. Sometimes protruding your jaw (like an under-bite) helps to put a little more pressure on the reed to stabilize the sound. It's up to you to see what works for each fingering. As you build upon your multiphonic vocabulary, begin to add variations of articulations as you hold the sound for an extra challenge.

Remember that ANY fingering can produce a multiphonic if so intended. Knowing this, what other multiphonic fingerings can you find? Through patience, a new palette of sound could very well reveal itself to you. As you may have noticed, changing just one finger can produce dramatically exciting results.

Record some of your own, personal multiphonic findings in the key diagrams provided:

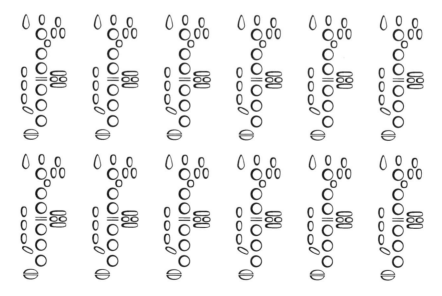

VOCALIZATIONS

Vocalizing into the saxophone is a deeply intimate experience. I remember seeing a concert where a saxophonist unclipped his horn, turned it around and began to scream into the bell of his horn. My jaw fell to the floor. I was speechless and had never seen a saxophonist do anything like that before. "Is he crazy?" Was the question I asked myself. It wasn't until years later that I realized what a personal statement that performance was, and how intense of an urge it must have been for him to commit to such a performance, not to mention with such intensity—the band soared to new heights. It was one of the most memorable concerts I have ever experienced.

Singing while holding a tone requires you to sing (or 'hum') into the saxophone, holding a pitch steady with your voice while playing a note on your horn at the same time. To begin practicing this, start warming up your voice by singing a tone, let's choose a C for this example, and hold it very steady. Sing it strongly and with good volume and air support, as you will need this strength when you incorporate your voice with your instrument. Exhale completely. Inhale to prepare for humming another C. While humming, bring the instrument to a comfortable height and playing position and play a C in the same range that you are humming (octave displacement is fine). Hold the feeling of unison as closely as possible between your voice and the instrument. Tune your voice to your instrument. This will likely feel very shaky and uncomfortable at first, and that's okay. You may feel your entire head vibrating with the sound since there are a lot of opposing forces at work. Once you have a feeling for this sensation, hold that same C in your voice and change the note that's played on your instrument, thereby creating an interval between your singing voice and the fingering on the instrument. Hold the tone steady with your voice, and be wary of the natural tendency to go flat. Stay strong.

Explore several different intervallic combinations, but keep going back to that steady tone in unison and that feeling of playing and singing in-tune simultaneously. Let that be your benchmark. Here is an example to get you started:

1) Hold your voice on a single tone while you play that same tone:

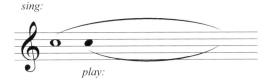

While you sing through your horn, experiment raising and lowering your voice ever so slightly, to the point where you're creating a small polyphonic interval, or a 'false' multiphonic.

2) Hold your voice on a single tone, while playing different pitches:

🔊 VOCALIZATIONS A

Track 16

The next step is to challenge your voice by increasing the range in which you sing into the horn. Try singing and humming using your 'falsetto' voice for men, or your 'head voice' for women. I believe you will find a new area of resistance to work with. Apply your slow and methodical practices to this new and challenging territory.

Growling

The 'growling' vocalization effect is much simpler to induce. All that one does to induce the growling effect is to vibrate the uvula at the back of your mouth (The uvula is that little thing that hangs in between your tonsils at the top of your throat). Think of what goes on when you gargle water. The action is very similar to that, but this time you're creating the 'gargled-water' sound without the use of any water:

 VOCALIZATIONS B
Track 17

Practice growling in a comfortable mid-range on your instrument. When it begins to feel comfortable, move higher up the range of the horn. Note that as you ascend the instrument, the shape of your throat changes, and so does your uvula's freedom to vibrate. This means that it becomes a subtler, and consequently more difficult action to produce and control. Stick to the instrument's middle range in the beginning, and work your way out from that.

Singing into the body of your instrument is another form of vocalization. Remove the neck and mouthpiece from the instrument. Finger a low B♭, and sing a steady tone into the top opening of the body of the saxophone, where the neck connects to the rest of the horn. While holding this tone very steady with your voice, change the fingering; go back and forth between a low B♭ and a low C. What do you hear? How does it affect your voice and pitch? What changes are there in the timbre of the sound? The steadier you are with your voice, the more you can milk out some creative fingerings to produce different, offset timbre effects and nuances.

VOCALIZATIONS C
Track 18

The next idea is to try buzzing your lips together into the neck and body of the saxophone (without the mouthpiece), just like how a trumpet or trombonist would blow into their instrument. Hold the lip-buzzing steady and keep your lips pressed comfortably onto the top opening of the saxophone. Practice inducing the buzzing smoothly and with a great deal of control. Also experiment here with changing your fingerings while buzzing into the instrument to see what can be gained when many keys are depressed, or when many keys are open.

VOCALIZATIONS D

Track 18

26

'CROW' PITCHES

Playing pitches on the mouthpiece alone has been called many things; some I've heard are "buzzing the mouthpiece", "mouthpiece tones" and "crow pitches". I like the image of the crow (and all birds for that matter), hence the title of this exercise and technique.

Every mouthpiece is different, but generally speaking the following tones will be produced on a mouthpiece alone with a neutral embouchure:

Soprano Mouthpiece	Concert C
Alto Mouthpiece	Concert A
Tenor Mouthpiece	Concert G
Baritone Mouthpiece	Concert D

First, begin by simply holding steady a neutral tone. This is not as easy as it sounds! Practice this with a tuner, and aim for a complete in-tune-ness with the tone. Remember to avoid any 'biting' of your lips and/or jaw.

After you feel steady, hold another tone steadily, perhaps moving a whole-step up or whole-step down from the neutral tone. Take frequent breaks and with that, full and relaxed breaths.

After you can play a few crow pitches in tune with a tuner, try practicing a few scales. Our goal is to gain control over about an octave's worth of range using just the mouthpiece. This will be more attainable on a baritone mouthpiece than on a soprano mouthpiece, as the chamber of the mouthpiece is larger, and therefore can produce a wider range of pitch.

 'CROW' PITCHES A
Track 20

Begin by practicing the major scale in crow-pitch tones, carefully and in-tune, then branch out and explore other parallel modes. Here are some to practice on the mouthpiece, notated in the key of C for demonstration purposes:

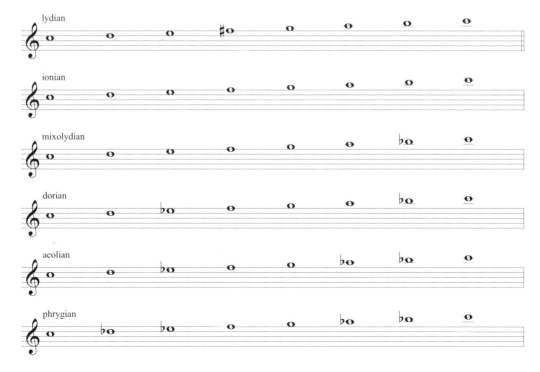

Now attach the mouthpiece to the neck of the saxophone (but still without the saxophone body) and play a tone.

'CROW' PITCHES B
Track 21

Place one of your thumbs about a fingernail's length into the hollow end of the neck, and play the neck as if it were a slide whistle. Observe how the pitch changes as you move your thumb further in or further out of the neck. Take a moment now to see how far you can go to play melodies with this new technique. Explore different articulations. Explore different jaw positions, throat shapes and sub-toning. Explore the potential of this new instrument, which was somehow before hidden in plain sight.

RHYTHMIC KEY CLICKS

By clicking the keys of the saxophone, we can transform ourselves as saxophonists into rhythmic, tonal percussionists.

Observe the sound of the rhythmic pitch of the different fingering combinations in the following examples. Note heads with 'ø' indicate an open fingering. Note heads with an 'x' indicate a closed fingering.

 RHYTHMIC KEY CLICKS

When we just play the keys, we liberate ourselves from needing both our hands to play just one note, and in only

left hand:

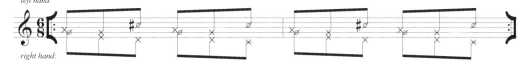

right hand:

one rhythm. This way our digits are free to execute multiple independent rhythms in with each other:
Also try displacing the following left hand rhythm to all different parts of the beat.

left hand:

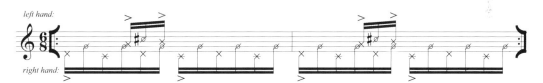

right hand:

Playing two rhythms across two hands may seem rather unfamiliar to us as saxophonists, since we primarily focus ourselves with playing with two hands for one note. In this regard, this exercise is also a practice of rhythmic independence. Practicing the rhythms found in snare drum studies can be a tremendous resource to open us up to this new practice:

Apply this rhythmic key click practice to the rhythm piece of music you're working on, distributing the rhythms

left hand:

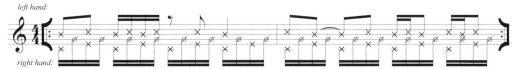

right hand:

across a variety of fingerings (not just the pitches indicated on the sheet music). Come up with some of your own rhythms to practice, spending a good amount of time working out two rhythms in sync with both hands:

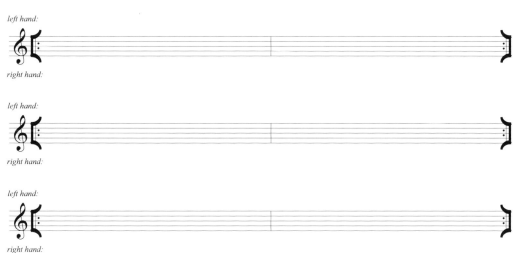

Circular breathing is the practice of pushing air out through one's throat and cheeks while simultaneously inhaling, thus producing a constant sound and airflow through the instrument. At first thought this may seem tremendously out of reach, but it is actually one of the more easy to obtain extended techniques, and is available to all wind instrumentalists. It is an ancient skill that glass blowers and musicians have perfected for centuries. Now it's your turn.

Below is an exercise that, once mastered, will result in multiple benefits. Not only does it teach you the technique of circular breathing, but it also doubles as an excellent tool for embouchure strengthening.

1) Find a medium sized balloon. (Any conventional party balloon is fine.)

2) Fill the balloon to a maximum of ⅓ in capacity, and simply hold it in place in your embouchure for as long as possible. Do *not* close off the balloon's opening; instead, hold it firmly in place using only the strength of your lip muscles. Think of your lips as an elastic band that's fully encompassing the nozzle of balloon, not favoring any pressure from any one side. Hold it steadily in place; strong and yet relaxed is the sensation we're after. Within about 20-30 seconds, you should feel the muscles at the sides of your mouth starting to 'burn' with the intensity of this strengthening exercise. Keep your eye brows and other facial muscles relaxed. Please don't hold your breath, as that also creates an unnecessary tension. Practice this many times.

3) Once your embouchure is holding the semi-inflated balloon calmly and securely, begin to breathe in and out through your nose in a relaxed manner, while maintaining the strength of your mouth and lips.

4) Begin again in the same way by inflating the balloon to no more than ⅓ capacity; hold it securely in your embouchure and ensure that no air is escaping through the sides of your mouth. Inflate your cheeks to take in some of the air from the balloon, and simply push the air inside your mouth back into the balloon using only your cheek muscles, without swallowing any air from the balloon, and without blowing any extra air into the balloon using your diaphragm. We are isolating the muscle group in your face—your cheeks and only your cheeks—to push air back and forth from your mouth to the balloon and vice versa.

5) Continue the movement as outlined in step 4, but this time add little inhales and exhales in and out through your nose while gently 'pushing' air back and forth between your cheeks and the balloon.

Keep practicing this exercise with the balloon to build up strength with your cheek muscles. I like to do it when traveling, or when I'm forced to be away from the instrument to still maintain a practice of control, strength and physicality in my embouchure. Without this strength, you will not be able to have enough control to push the air and maintain constant sound, hence the importance of training against the resistance that the balloon provides. (Be sure to discard your balloon every week or two if you've been practicing regularly, as it will quickly lose its beautiful elasticity and other resistant qualities.)

....

Once you have maintained a steady airflow away from the instrument, it can be very difficult to transfer the practice to the horn. Experiment with placing the air in different places in the cheeks and don't be discouraged if the tone is not steady at all. Practice being happy when you can hold a pitch for a short while!

Try to apply a circular breath to the saxophone while holding a note in a comfortable middle-range tone on the instrument:

Next, apply a circular breath to a slow trill or simple finger movement:

Finally, apply a circular breath to a musical passage or repertoire excerpt:

 CIRCULAR BREATHING

Track 23

'PREPARING' THE SAXOPHONE

Preparing the saxophone essentially means modifying the instrument by adding materials to its mechanics. For example, some classical saxophonists insert a narrow, donut-shaped, felt-covered 'mute' into the bell of the saxophone to absorb certain harsh, bright resonances. I have also known free jazz musicians to plug the bell of their horn with a large, industrial-sized drain stopper, which gives them more pressure and resistance in the air column to play with. One may also use a piece of cork, (easy to find from any bottle of wine) to clamp the low C key permanently closed. I have even known saxophonists to play with a certain amount of water intentionally trapped in their instrument, or attach little bells and rattles to various keys in order to maximize the amount of noise or buzz that their instrument can produce. The sky is the limit.

Something to try yourself: Unclip your neckstrap from the horn, and gently rub the end of the neckstrap onto the keys, thereby producing a controlled percussive rattle-like sound.

 PREPARATIONS
Track 24

Another simple preparation you can try is to find a different style reed to play. For instance, if you play the alto, try a tenor reed on your alto mouthpiece; if you play tenor, find a baritone reed; if you play soprano, find an alto reed. Keep in mind that you may need to use a slightly larger ligature to accommodate the larger reed.

Here are some common household objects that can be used to experiment with in 'preparing' the saxophone:

LOW A

Perhaps one of the first 'extended' techniques taught to saxophonists is how to play a low A on the alto and tenor saxophone. All you must do is play a low B♭ with confidence and cover off half of the bell with your left inner thigh. You must turn your body somewhat awkwardly in order to perform it. Practice going from a low B♭ to a low A while sitting down, that way it'll be more convenient to turn the instrument into your leg to get the low A when you want it. After you hear the pitch drop a full semitone, try to play a low A while standing as well.

Practice playing between low B♭ and low A, slowly:

 LOW A

Track 25

EPILOGUE

What is the tradition of the saxophone?

The saxophone was invented in the mid-19th century and because of this, it's very much considered a modern instrument, and somewhat of a lone wolf among the longstanding, orchestral instrumental establishment. This puts the saxophone into a rather young, interesting and unsure place in the history of music. Although this territory may seem daunting, it's also ripe with possibility, as there were no formal conventions or methods for saxophone performance until very recently in modern history. Because of this, every great saxophonist has tailored the performance of the instrument exactly to his/her needs, basing their creative direction solely on their personal interests and fiery curiosity. What I hope to have expressed within these pages is a sense of the pioneering feeling of the very first saxophonists, and their humble inventor Mr. Adolphe Sax, who were so enthralled with the idea of manifesting a new, exciting and exotic sound into the world.

I employ you, faithful reader, to listen to every saxophonist that you can. Each one of these texts is a wealth of specialized information for further in-depth study. Listen to every saxophonist you can. Listen to the birds, wind and the ocean. Let it inspire you. I believe that any true, personal sound that one has embraced may indeed be called 'extended'. In the end, it matters very little how many multiphonics you can play. What matters more is the practice, the listening and the experience; what that teaches you is most important. Embrace the unknown, and carry your findings to the surface so that others may know it too. Play it loudly. Invent, innovate and share the sound of your introspective practice with others. May this be the tradition of our instrument.

Blank Manuscript: